The Story of
OLYMPIC SWIMMER
DUKE KAHANAMOKU

by **Ellie Crowe**
with illustrations by **Richard Waldrep**

Lee & Low Books Inc.
New York

To Micah, Luke, and Sydney,
who love riding the blue waves of Hawai'i —E.C.

To my daughter, Madeline, Maddy, "Maddo" —R.W.

Text from *Surfer of the Century the Life of Duke Kahanamoku* copyright © 2010 by Ellie Crowe
Sidebar text by Ellie Crowe copyright © 2018 by Lee & Low Books Inc.
Illustrations from *Surfer of the Century the Life of Duke Kahanamoku*
copyright © 2010 by Richard Waldrep
p. 14: Glasshouse Images/Everett Collection.
p. 24: Image by KDS444, used under a Creative Commons Attribution-Share Alike 4.0
International license, https://commons.wikimedia.org/wiki/File:Surfboard.svg.
p. 31: public domain
p. 41: Library of Congress, Prints & Photographs Division, photograph by Harris & Ewing,
LC-DIG-hec-13257
p. 43: Library of Congress, Prints & Photographs Division, LC-DIG-ggbain-25203
p. 53: Beata Jancsik / Shutterstock.com

Manufactured in the United States of America by Lake Book Manufacturing, Inc.
Edited by Louise May and Kandace Coston
Book design by NeuStudio
Book production by The Kids at Our House

The text is set in Vollkorn
The display font is set in Avenir Next
The illustrations are rendered in acrylic on canvas

10 9 8 7 6 5 4 3 2 1
First Edition
Cataloging-in-Publication data is on file with the Library of Congress.
ISBN 978-1-62014-852-5

TABLE OF CONTENTS

CHAPTER ONE
STAR SWIMMER

*S*urf's up!

Eager surfers gripped their wooden surfboards and stared out at the monster waves. Spawned far out at sea, the thirty-foot "Bluebirds" streaked across miles of ocean in a solid line, crashing in white foam on Waikiki Beach. Such huge waves occurred only on extraordinary occasions, the result of underwater earthquakes or volcanic eruptions. Who dared surf the Bluebirds?

Only one surfer mastered the gigantic waves that day in 1917—Duke Kahanamoku. He rode a thundering Bluebird for almost two miles, from the deep blue ocean to the white sand beach.

The Pacific Ocean was Duke's backyard. Born in 1890 in Honolulu, on the Hawaiian island of Oʻahu, Duke Paoa Kahanamoku lived with his family across the road from Waikiki Beach. Duke's childhood was filled with *aloha*. His parents were loving and supportive. He had five brothers, three sisters, and more than thirty cousins with whom to play. Neighbors helped one another and got together often, sharing the bananas, coconuts, taro, and sweet potatoes they grew in their gardens and the fish, crabs, squid, and octopuses they caught in the ocean.

aloha: love, kindness, grace, affection, compassion; also a traditional Hawaiian greeting and farewell

When he was four years old, Duke learned to swim in the old Hawaiian way. His father and uncle took him in an outrigger canoe, tied a rope around his waist, and tossed him into the ocean. Wiggling like a little tadpole, Duke made his way back to the canoe.

Duke's mother told him never to be afraid of the water and to go out as far as he wanted. His father said the mighty shark was their family's Hawaiian guardian and would protect him. Swimming each day, Duke soon learned to surf, dive, and hold his breath underwater for minutes at a time.

In school Duke struggled with his lessons, but in the ocean he was a star. As soon as the school bell rang, he raced to the beach and dived into the blue waves. The ocean was a second home to Duke, and he was happiest when he was swimming.

By the time he was a teenager, Duke was a very fast swimmer. His tall, strong body was designed for swimming. His large hands scooped through the water, while his big feet, like fins, **propelled** him along.

Duke had a natural talent, and he was determined to use it. He wanted to win races. He wanted to be a champion swimmer. Many of his friends could swim fast. The difference between swimming fast and winning races would be dedication and hard work.

Duke pushed himself to get better, swimming miles through the ocean day after day until his arm and leg muscles burned. He dropped out of high school and started working on the beach, making and selling surfboards. He earned enough money to help pay his family's bills, and

he had plenty of time to swim. Soon Duke swam faster than all his friends, and he longed for an opportunity to race the best swimmers from the mainland United States.

When several top Australian swimmers visited Hawai'i in 1910, Duke studied their special crawl stroke. Deciding that their stiff-legged kick used up too much energy, Duke developed the flutter kick, a **flexible**-knee version of the Australian crawl. He called his new swimming style the Hawaiian crawl and joked that his kick was the Kahanamoku kick.

One afternoon in the summer of 1911, Bill Rawlins, a Honolulu **attorney** with an interest in swimming, was watching Duke slash through the ocean. He couldn't believe how fast the young man swam. Fetching a stopwatch, he asked Duke and two of his friends to swim a measured 100-yard course. When Rawlins timed the swimmers, he was stunned. Duke had shown amazing speed. Rawlins thought Duke had the makings of a swimming champion.

"I'd like to coach you," Rawlins told Duke.

Duke's heart leaped. "It's a deal if you think I've got it," he said.

They closed the agreement with a handshake and a smile.

A Brief History of Hawai'i

Around 400 A.D., daring Polynesian voyagers left their home on the Marquesas Islands in the southern Pacific Ocean and sailed 2,500 miles to the isolated and sparsely populated islands of Hawai'i. A second wave of voyagers arrived from Tahiti around 1,000 A.D. These new arrivals formed a highly class-conscious society under chiefs who claimed to be **descendants** of the gods. Citizens were governed by a strict system of laws known as *kapu*, which is often translated as "forbidden." The harsh *kapu* system protected the power of the rulers and kept order among the people by tightly managing their everyday lives. The penalty for breaking any of the numerous *kapu* laws was death. Peace on the islands was also frequently shattered by battles between warring chiefs of the different islands.

In 1778, Europeans, led by British explorer Captain James Cook, arrived in Hawai'i on high-masted sailing ships. Soon more travelers arrived, hoping to profit from Hawai'i's sandalwood, whales, and fertile land. The introduction of European military weapons to Hawai'i

helped the **ambitious** young King Kamehameha con-
quer and unite the islands, establishing the Kingdom
of Hawai'i in 1783.

Immigration to Hawai'i continued to increase
throughout the 1800s as the US and other neighboring
countries took greater interest in the islands. From
the United States came missionaries and American
businessmen who bought land to grow vast fields of
sugarcane and pineapple. Waves of immigrants from
Japan, China, and the Philippines arrived to work in the
fields, changing the racial makeup of the islands. More
than half the native population succumbed to diseases
like smallpox brought by the new arrivals.

The US recognized the benefits of Hawai'i's agri-
culture and strategic military location in the Pacific and
challenged Hawai'i's government for greater control of
its resources. White American businessmen with finan-
cial interests in Hawai'i pushed for a new constitution
that would reduce the power of Hawai'i's monarch, give
the right to vote to more white Americans, and weaken
the voting power of native Hawaiians and Asian immigrants. Hawai'i's leader, King Kalākaua, was forced to
sign the new constitution at gunpoint. This legislation

became known as the Bayonet Constitution.

King Kalākaua's sister, Liliuokalani, took the throne after his death in 1891 and tried to restore royal power in 1893, but she clashed with the American businessmen who wished to protect their power within Hawai'i's government. The Queen was placed under house arrest and the Republic of Hawai'i was formed. In 1898, Hawai'i became a territory of the United States. In 1959, Hawai'i officially became the 50th state of the US.

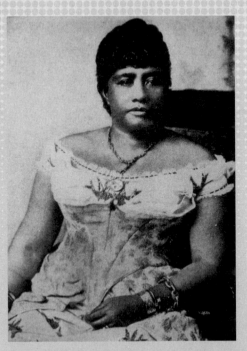

Queen Liliuokalani during her reign, 1891-1893.

CHAPTER TWO

RECORD BREAKER

Duke and his two friends joined with other eager swimmers to form a swim team. Rawlins told the group that to get **recognition** for any records they set, they had to belong to a surf club. Duke had tried earlier to join the

Healani Club and had been refused membership even though he knew some of the members. To the club he was just a penniless beachboy. Duke was hurt but managed to shrug off the rejection.

Acting on Rawlins's advice, the members of the swimming team organized the Hui Nalu, Club of the Waves. They called it the "poor man's surf club" because they had no clubhouse and met under a *hau* tree at Waikiki Beach.

Sitting in the shade of the tree, Duke and his friends worked on building bigger surfboards with sleeker lines and better balance. Duke developed a huge, 16-foot, 114-pound board that handled well. In Waikiki's rolling waves, the beachboys worked on new surfing **maneuvers**: standing on a board backward, stepping from board to board, sliding left and right with the waves, doing headstands, and riding **tandem** with another person, usually a pretty girl, on the surfer's shoulders.

In 1910, Hawai'i's sports clubs had voted to form the Hawaiian Amateur Athletic Union (AAU). The creation of the AAU-Hawai'i made

Hawaiian athletes eligible for national Amateur Athletic Union events and possible participation in the Olympics.

The AAU-Hawai'i decided to hold its first contest, a swim meet, on August 12, 1911. This was Duke's big chance. He would compete against nationally ranked swimmers from the mainland United States.

The race meant a lot to Hawai'i. There were many gifted watermen on the islands, but no Hawaiian had ever been recognized by the world as a top swimming champion. Rawlins was confident Duke could beat the swimmers from the mainland and make it onto the US team for the 1912 **Olympic Games** in Stockholm, Sweden.

On the day of the swim meet, excited spectators gathered at Honolulu's **wharves**. Hawai'i did not have an Olympic-sized swimming pool, so the contest was held in the ocean, with the swimmers racing between two piers in the harbor. The crowd hummed with eager anticipation as the start of the 100-yard freestyle race grew near.

Heart thudding, Duke stood at the edge of the wharf.

BAM! The pistol shot rang out.

Duke's family and friends screamed his name as the swimmers hit the water. They were neck and neck until Duke, fierce with determination, forged ahead. He plowed through the water like a speedboat, a mound of water rising in front of his chest, a white wake of foam trailing behind him. Duke shot to the finish line with lightning speed.

Pulling himself out of the water, Duke was puzzled by the judges' startled expressions. Then they shouted that Duke had broken the world record! He had swum the race in 55.4 seconds, shaving 4.6 seconds off the official time. Duke grinned, shaking his head in amazement. The cheering spectators hugged him and clapped his back. Everyone wanted to touch him, be a part of his success.

By the end of the day, Duke had shattered three long-standing AAU freestyle swimming records: the 100-yard, the 50-yard, and the 220-yard. The judges declared that his times were fast enough to **qualify** for the Olympic tryouts.

Duke was bursting with excitement. How great it would be to compete in the Olympics and bring home the gold for Hawai'i!

For weeks news reporters followed Duke around the beach at Waikiki, taking his photo and trying to interview him. The reporters found it difficult to get Duke to say much. He was too shy and humble to talk about himself.

Then bad news arrived. Duke's new records were so amazing, Amateur Athletic Union officials in New York refused to believe his times. "What are you using for stopwatches?" a **sarcastic** official asked. "Alarm clocks?"

Duke was shattered. He feared everything was over. Trying to drown his disappointment, Duke grabbed his surfboard and headed to the ocean. "Coming down!" he yelled as he launched his board over the crests of the waves. His friends made way for him. They knew how he felt.

Meanwhile, word of Duke's record-breaking swimming times had swept the athletic

world. AAU officials, curious about the young, untrained swimmer, wanted to see Duke swim for themselves. They invited him to the mainland to try out for the United States Olympic team.

Thrilled by the news, Duke and his family huddled around the kitchen table. Money was tight. They didn't know how they would pay for Duke's boat trip to California. Soon friends and supporters gathered to help. Coach Rawlins arranged benefit potluck dinners and made generous donations. Duke's friends raised cash by performing a play on the deck of an abandoned ship. Along with **contributions** from others, enough money was raised to send Duke to the mainland.

How Surfboards Are Made

The surfboard and the sport of surfing are believed to have originated in Polynesia as early as 400 A.D. Early Hawaiian surfboards were made of wood from trees on the islands. These wooden surfboards ranged from 12 to 16 feet long and weighed between 77 to 150 lbs. Boards were shaped with a small hand tool of sharpened stone called an adze, smoothed with coral or rough stones, and stained with pounded kukui tree bark, which gave the board a water-resistant surface. These early surfboards did not have fins, so surfers had to drag their rear foot in the water to change direction and angle across the face of a wave. The first fixed fin was created in 1935 by surfing pioneer Tom Blake. It revolutionized surfing because it made it easier for surfers to pivot in the water.

In the 1940s, the popularization of fiberglass, a material made of reinforced plastic, meant that surfboards could be made stronger, lightweight, and waterproof. Modern surfboards are shaped from long boards called blanks, which are made of Styrofoam, epoxy, or polyurethane. Big factories may use machines to cut blanks into surfboards, while a surfboard shaper working on a smaller scale may custom-shape it by hand. The blank is then buffed to make the surfaces even. Once the desired form is reached, the blank is split from nose to tail and a wooden strip called a "stringer" is glued between the two halves. This strengthens the board and reduces the chance of it snapping under a big wave. The surfboard is then spray-painted and laminated and a fin is attached.

Surfboard builders continue to experiment with board construction and design as surfers search for that "perfect board."

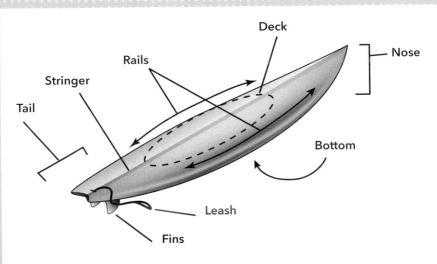

Diagram of a modern surfboard.

CHAPTER THREE
SETBACKS AND SUCCESS

Filled with Olympic dreams, Duke said good-bye to family and friends and boarded an ocean steamer to California in early February 1912. Rawlins's work as an attorney kept him from traveling, so Duke was **accompanied** by two members of his swim team. Lew Henderson acted as manager and Dude Miller was the swimming trainer.

In Los Angeles, Duke stared wide-eyed at the crowded streets. This big city was very different from his island home. Reporters described Duke as a strange-looking, dark-skinned native from distant lands. People stared at him. Restaurant waiters pretended not to see him. After a few awkward meals, Duke decided to eat alone in his hotel room so that Henderson and Miller would not be embarrassed by his presence.

Duke's first qualifying race was in Chicago. When he got off the train from Los Angeles, the icy winter wind bit through his thin suit coat. Looking for a way to stay warm, Duke stuffed cardboard under his coat and kept it tightly buttoned. The cardboard was secret until Duke unthinkingly pulled off his coat in the changing room of the Chicago swim stadium. Everyone laughed as the cardboard fell to the floor.

Duke burned with embarrassment but told himself to focus on the swimming. He knew he was as good as any swimmer alive. Duke won the 100-yard freestyle race in 57 seconds. He was on his way to being accepted for the Olympic team.

Pittsburgh was even colder than Chicago. Upon arriving, Duke hurried into a restaurant to order a bowl of hot soup. The waiter took one look at Duke's dark skin and asked him to leave. **Humiliated**, he headed for the door.

Just then someone called, "Hello, Duke! How about joining us?" Duke turned to see a friend who visited Hawai'i every few years. People were staring, but his friend said, "Waiter, please have another place set at my table for the **sensational**

Hawaiian swimmer, Duke Kahanamoku." Duke downed his food as fast as he could. He thanked his friend and his friend's companions, invited them to visit him in Hawai'i, and hurriedly left the restaurant.

That night in the Pittsburgh stadium Duke was tense with anticipation.

He was competing against world-class swimmers, and every one of them wanted a place on the Olympic team. Duke dived into the pool, ready to prove himself. The water was freezing. His left leg cramped, and to his horror Duke found he couldn't swim. He came to a crippled halt and had to be pulled from the pool. Surrounded by the booing crowd, Duke looked down sadly at his big, cold feet. He had always thought he could depend on his body, but this time it had failed him.

The next day, Duke decided to swim around the pool before his first race to get his body used to the icy temperature. The crowd jeered, calling him a show-off. Duke tried to ignore the taunts. He climbed out of the pool and stood alone, waiting for the other swimmers to line up. His mind went back home. He thought of all the people who had paid for his trip, and his family, friends, and coach, who were praying for him to succeed. He couldn't disappoint them.

From the moment Duke hit the water, he

swam with spectacular speed. Used to open-ocean racing, he lost time on turns, but made up the loss with his furious arm strokes and powerful flutter kicks. He won the 100-yard race and then the 50-yard race, beating the world records with seconds to spare. Now on his side, the spectators screamed their support.

The endless swimming and hard work had paid off. Duke was going to the Olympic Games in Stockholm! He would be the first Hawaiian ever to swim in the Olympics, competing against the strongest swimmers from around the world. The competition would be fierce, but Duke ached to test himself against these legendary athletes.

The Olympic Games

The Olympic Games are an international sports festival that began in Ancient Greece. The original Games were dedicated to the Greek gods (who were said to live on Mount Olympus) and were staged on the plains of Olympia, Greece, every fourth year for several hundred years. The Games were abolished as a **"pagan cult"** in the early Christian era.

It would be another 1,500 years before the Games would rise again, largely thanks to the efforts of Baron Pierre de Coubertin of France. Dedicated to the

A 2013 Russian postage stamp with the image of Baron Pierre de Coubertin.

promotion of physical education, the young baron was inspired to create a modern Olympic Games after visiting the ancient Olympic site. In 1892, at a gathering of the French Union of Athletic Sports Societies, Coubertin introduced the idea of the Olympics as an international athletic competition with athletes from different countries competing. Two years later, he organized a meeting, bringing together 79 delegates from 12 countries. They established the first International Olympic (IOC) and the framework of games being held every four years.

The first modern Olympics took place in 1896 in Athens, Greece. The athletes, all men, competed in 43 events, covering track and field, cycling, swimming, gymnastics, weightlifting, wrestling, fencing, shooting, and tennis. All subsequent Olympiads have been numbered even when no Games take place, as in 1916, during World War I, and in 1940 and 1944, during World War II. The Winter Olympics debuted in 1924. Since 1994, the Summer and Winter Olympic Games have been held separately and have alternated every two years. The Summer Games, with its wide array of events, are still the focal point of the modern Olympics.

The Olympic Games have changed radically over the years. In the first modern Olympics, 14 nations were represented. In 2016, 206 countries took part. The number of athletes participating grew from 246 in 1896 to 10,000 in 2016, while the number of spectators has grown from 80,000 to over 1.17 million. In 1896, there were 43 events; in 2016 there were 306. Only five sports have been contested at every summer Olympic Games: athletics, cycling, fencing, gymnastics and swimming.

The Games are governed by the International Olympic Committee (IOC), whose headquarters is in Lausanne, Switzerland.

CHAPTER FOUR
THE 1912 OLYMPICS

The Olympic ship, the SS *Finland,* arrived in Sweden in July 1912. The sky was overcast and the water looked dark and cold. Crowds of reporters rushed the athletes as they milled around on the ship's deck. The reporters had many names for Duke—human fish, half-man-half-fish, merman, paddlewheel steamer—and they showered him with questions about his amazing speed. Duke answered the reporters' questions as best he could.

Escaping to the top deck, Duke found a sheltered spot and sat talking with a new friend, Native American track-and-field star Jim Thorpe. Like Duke, Jim was a natural athlete, **virtually** self-trained. They had both made it onto the Olympic team at a time when people of color rarely competed for the United States.

"Jimmy," Duke said, "you can run, jump, throw things, and carry the ball. You do everything. So why don't you swim, too?"

"Duke, I saved that for you to take care of," Jim said, grinning.

Summers in Sweden have almost twenty-four hours of daylight, and Duke found it hard to get enough sleep at night. So on the morning of his first race, he decided to take a nap in his cabin.

Crowds had gathered at the Stockholm Olympic swimming venue. The Swedish royal family, diplomats, military officers, and thousands of fans were there to watch the popular 100-meter freestyle race.

"Kahanamoku wanted on the starting platform," an official announced over the public address system. After a few moments the official repeated loudly, "Kahanamoku wanted on the starting platform."

Duke did not appear. Frantically his teammates searched the swimming stadium. Then they raced to the ship and searched there. Michael McDermott, the US breaststroke champion, found Duke and shook him awake.

At the stadium, Duke pushed through the crowds and approached the starting official.

"Where've you been?" the frowning official demanded.

"I'm—I'm sorry," Duke apologized. "I've been sleeping."

The official told him he was too late.

Silence fell on the crowd. Duke thought he would die. Everything he had worked so hard for—gone in an instant. He had missed his race in the Olympics!

Suddenly, Cecil Healy, Australia's star swimmer, called out for Duke to be allowed in the race. Healy refused to swim unless Duke competed, even though Duke was his main threat.

It seemed as though no one in the stadium breathed. Duke stared at the ground and waited for a minute that seemed to go on forever.

Finally the official relented, giving Duke a curt nod.

Adrenaline pumping through his body, Duke lined up with Bretting and Ramme from Germany, Longworth and Healy from Australia, and Huszagh from the United States. The starting pistol cracked, and the six swimmers hit the water. Duke was up first from his dive, slicing through the water. At twenty-five meters, Duke was well ahead. Then from the corner of his eye he saw Healy coming up fast. Duke powered on, ripping across the pool, his body lifting up and forward. The crowd roared. With Healy on his heels, Duke slammed the finish line, clocking 63.4 seconds, a new Olympic record. Healy was 1.2 seconds behind. Duke had won Olympic gold!

King Gustav of Sweden was so impressed with Duke that he personally awarded him the gold medal and placed the wreath of victory on his head. Duke smiled and **stammered** his thanks. His smile grew wider when the king also honored Duke's friend Jim Thorpe, who had won two gold medals.

Jim Thorpe

Born in Oklahoma in 1887, James Francis Thorpe was a member of the Sac and Fox Nation. His name in the Sac language, Wa-Tho-Huk, translates as "path lit by great flash of lightning" or, more simply, "Bright Path." Thorpe's athletic abilities showed at an early age. He and his twin brother, Charlie, rode horses and went trapping, hunting, and shooting with their father on thirty-mile treks into the wilderness.

At age six, Thorpe and Charlie were sent to a Native American boarding school where they were supposed to learn how to read, write, and integrate with white American society. Much of the educational process at these institutions involved stripping Native American students of their culture. At the Agency Boarding School, Thorpe was physically **reprimanded** if he spoke Sac, and his classes kept him inside, away from the outdoors he enjoyed. He found being cut off from his family and their way of life very difficult.

A few years later, Charlie died of pneumonia, leaving Thorpe heartbroken. Thorpe wanted to move back home, but his parents believed it was important he be educated, so they sent him to a school called the Haskell Institute in Lawrence, Kansas. Haskell was a better fit for Thorpe. There he studied engineering and took an interest in sports.

When Thorpe was sixteen, he was recruited to attend Carlisle Indian Industrial School, a **vocational** school for Native Americans in Pennsylvania. Thorpe was strolling across the Carlisle campus one day when he saw student athletes practicing the high jump. Thorpe was then 5-foot-8, and the bar the students were jumping over was set at 5-9. On his first try, he cleared the high jump bar! When he was summoned to the office of the school's renowned football and track coach, Glenn "Pop" Warner, Thorpe thought he was in trouble. But Warner told him he'd broken the school record and asked him to join the track team.

At Carlisle, Thorpe excelled in football, baseball, track, lacrosse, hockey, handball, tennis, and boxing. He even won the ballroom dancing championship! Football was his favorite sport. He matured to almost six feet tall and 185 pounds and led Carlisle to outstanding football seasons in 1911 and 1912. In the spring of 1912, Thorpe started training for the 1912

Summer Olympics in Stockholm, Sweden. He practiced hurdles, the shot put, pole vaulting, javelin, discus, hammer, and 56-lb. weight lifting. A hardworking and dedicated athlete, Thorpe was on his way to glory.

Thorpe playing football.

Thorpe was the first Native American to win an Olympic gold medal for the US. He won four of the five events in the **pentathlon** and finished third in the fifth event, a record unequaled to this day. When awarding Thorpe his gold medals, King Gustav of Sweden said, "Sir, you are the greatest athlete in the world," to which Thorpe replied, "Thanks, King."

A year after the Olympics, it surfaced that Thorpe had played two semi-professional seasons of baseball. The Amateur Athletic Union withdrew his amateur status. The International Olympic Committee (IOC) had strict rules about Olympians receiving payment for participating in professional athletics. Despite the fact that Thorpe had been paid very little for playing baseball, the Committee declared him a professional and stripped him of his Olympic titles, medals, and awards.

Thorpe managed to move on after this devastating **ordeal**. He became a professional athlete and eventually played baseball for the New York Giants, the Cincinnati Reds, and the Boston Braves. Thorpe also played football for the Canton (Ohio) Bulldogs from 1915 until 1920 and the Cleveland Indians in 1921. He organized and coached the Oorang Indians, a professional football team comprised completely of American Indians. On August 20, 1920, the owners of four Ohio League teams met to form a professional football league. They nominated Jim Thorpe as its president, hoping that his fame would help their organization's credibility. The group evolved into today's National Football League (NFL). In 1950, Thorpe's athletic **prowess** earned him

Thorpe fielding a ball for New York Giants.

selection as the greatest athlete and the greatest football player of the twentieth century in an Associated
Press poll of sports writers and broadcasters.

Thorpe died in 1953 at age 64 after suffering a heart
attack. By the late 1980s, the IOC eased restrictions
on professional and semi-professional athletes participating in the Olympics. Thorpe's Olympic medals were
restored to him **posthumously** in 1982.

CHAPTER FIVE
MASTER SURFER

Suddenly Duke was an international champion, and sports fans everywhere wanted to see the big Hawaiian swim. Duke **obliged**, competing in swimming pools all over Europe and even in the Seine River in Paris. Back in the US, he taught swimmers on the East Coast to surf. Although public beaches and pools on the mainland were mostly closed to people of color, Duke's **exhibitions** were a first step toward integrating these facilities.

To the world, Duke became a symbol of Hawai'i. When newspapers reported that he was a descendant of ancient Polynesian kings, Duke modestly replied that he was just a beachboy from Waikiki. Duke also tried hard to present a good image and live up to people's expectations. He slipped up only once. Traveling on a slow-moving steamer, Duke found the sparkling ocean just too tempting. When the boat's engine stalled and was being repaired, he dived over the side for a quick swim. The rough sea quickly pulled Duke and the ship in opposite directions. Duke swam as hard as he could, but he couldn't make it back. With passengers yelling, "Man overboard!" he was rescued by a lifeboat.

Duke's return to Honolulu in October 1912 was **triumphant**. Thousands of supporters met the ship. Cannons boomed. Music filled the air. Duke's family and friends rushed the **gangway** and piled colorful leis around his neck. The sweet-smelling flowers reached right up to Duke's eyes. He had to peek over them to see the welcoming crowd.

Duke received offers to turn professional and be paid for competing in swimming meets. But the Olympic Games were open only to unpaid **amateurs**, so Duke refused. He wanted to compete in the 1916 Olympics in Berlin, Germany.

While he trained, Duke needed to earn a living. He didn't have many work-related skills. He had left school early, and the ocean was all he knew. Finally Duke found a job assisting surveyors in

the Honolulu Water Department. Each day after work he ran to Waikiki Beach to swim.

In late 1914, the Australian swim team was training **feverishly** for the Berlin Olympics. They invited Duke to Australia to compete in swim meets with them. They also wanted him to demonstrate his Hawaiian crawl and flutter kick. Duke accepted eagerly.

Arriving in Sydney, Duke was surprised by the enthusiastic reception he received from the Australians. He promised to do his best to please everybody. During his thirty-three race tour, the sports stadiums of Sydney, Melbourne, and

Brisbane were packed with appreciative crowds. Duke gave outstanding performances in race after race and laughed when he read news reports about his "unusually large pedal extremities," which gave power to his Kahanamoku kick. Duke's sportsmanship and good nature won him many new fans.

The Australians had been so welcoming and generous, Duke wanted to do something to repay them. Although some Australians knew about surfing before his visit, Duke noticed that they were not taking advantage of their wonderful, big surf. He thought this was very unusual. Hawaiians had been riding the waves for at least a thousand years. Duke decided he would introduce the Australians to board surfing, the sport of the ancient Hawaiian kings.

No surfboard was available, so Duke bought a sugar pine plank and spent a day shaping an 8-foot, 9-inch board. Word spread that the Hawaiian swimming champion was going to ride ocean waves on a board, and crowds of curious people gathered at Freshwater Beach in Sydney.

The amazed spectators cheered with delight as Duke rode the board down the long, steep face of a wave and across the cove, continually beating the break.

By the end of the day Duke had soared, glided,

drifted, and stood on his head, all while riding his surfboard. For a finale he invited a girl to sit on his shoulder, and they rode a wave to shore while the onlookers clapped and shouted loudly.

Back in Hawai'i Duke continued to train for the Olympics. When he wasn't swimming or working, Duke and his Hui Nalu friends could be found at Waikiki Beach, teaching visitors to surf. Surfing was catching on as a sport on the east and west coasts of the US, and Duke loved sharing the excitement of riding the waves.

Duke's dream of competing in the 1916 Berlin Olympics came to an end when the games were canceled due to World War I, which had been raging in Europe since 1914. When the US entered the war in 1917, Duke traveled throughout the mainland as a Red Cross volunteer in water safety and lifesaving techniques. He also competed with other swimmers to raise money for the Red Cross and to purchase US war bonds.

Duke was twenty-eight when the war ended in 1918, and some feared he was too old to compete in the 1920 Olympic Games in Antwerp, Belgium.

But Duke wasn't ready to give up. He trained and swam himself into top condition. Once again Duke won Olympic gold for the US, speeding through the water far ahead of his competitors and clocking 60.4 seconds for the 100-meter freestyle race. He won a second gold medal as a member of the 4 x 200-meter freestyle relay team. Duke was proud of his participation in the first Olympics in which athletes took an **oath** to compete "for the glory of sport."

How to Surf

Surfing is a great way to get out in the ocean and ride a wave. Here are some surf basics you need to know before you paddle out.

The best way to start is to take a surfing lesson or ask a surfing friend for help. Find a flat, sandy beach with a few surfers and plenty of room for your own area in the water. **Longboards** are often recommended for beginners because they are easier to use.

Once you have your longboard, lay it on the sand and practice "popping up"—a surfing technique used to transition from lying on the surfboard to standing on it. Popping up looks like an explosive pushup. To practice, lie face down on the board. Place your hands on the board in push-up position with your legs extended behind you. In one quick motion, push yourself up with your arms and plant your feet firmly on your board. Your front foot should be facing forward (parallel to the board), and back foot facing sideways (perpendicular to the board). Your back foot will typically be the same as your dominant hand.

Before entering the ocean, make sure your board is properly waxed to provide good traction and solid footing. You should also prepare your leash—the tether that connects you to your board—by plugging it securely into your board and strapping the other end to your ankle. The leash will prevent your board from getting away from you, and possibly hitting others while you are in the water. (Always make sure you have a lifeguard's supervision when swimming or surfing!)

Paddle Out: Walk the longboard out in the ocean until the water becomes waist deep. Point the nose of the board away from the shore, climb on, lie flat on your stomach, and paddle away from shore using the **crawl stroke**. Paddle out to a spot where small, foamy waves are forming.

Catch the Wave: On your first couple of waves, don't try to stand up on the board. Instead, focus on catching the whitewater—the tops of forming waves—and riding it. When you see a small wall of whitewater rolling your way, point your board toward the beach, lie flat on your stomach, and paddle fast! Remain flat on your stomach and glide on the wave to the shore. Then paddle back out and do it again.

Waves come in different shapes, sizes, and **frequencies.** Bigger waves usually follow a set of smaller waves. It's important to practice your timing when surfing. You need to catch a wave as it is still forming, so you have enough time to pop up onto your feet before the wave breaks and the cresting white-water carries your board to shore.

When you feel ready to stand up on your board and surf, choose your wave, point your board toward shore, and start paddling. Once the board begins riding on the wave, pop up in one quick motion and plant your feet firmly on your board, just like you practiced on the beach. Stay in a low crouch to keep your balance. Look ahead, stay focused, and let the wave carry you in to shore. You're surfing!

A young surfer riding a wave.

Falling Off Your Board: When you fall off your board—and you will!—always try to fall backward and away from the surfboard, so the surfboard is not in the wave behind you. Falling backward also helps you to avoid crashing headfirst into anything that might be below the surface. Swim upward gently and feel what's ahead of you to avoid getting hit in the head by the board. You will fall off the first few times, but don't be discouraged. Even great surfers like **Kelly Slater** fall. Keep trying—there's nothing like the feeling of surfing a wave!

CHAPTER SIX
HAWAIIAN HERO

After Antwerp, the US Olympic team toured Europe and the United States. Duke was mobbed wherever he went. He was so popular that a **chaperone** was appointed to protect him from adoring fans.

In 1922 Duke moved to California. He appeared in several Hollywood movies, usually playing "native chiefs" because he was dark skinned. Duke always performed with dignity but wished directors would sometimes cast him in roles that were not such stereotypes.

When not acting, Duke took part in swimming exhibitions and gave surfing demonstrations across the country. He experimented with surfboard design and worked on making hollow boards. He also made himself a small, light board that he took everywhere.

Duke held the record as the fastest swimmer in the world for twelve years. When the 1924

Olympic Games in Paris, France, came up, he was determined to remain the champion despite strong competition from the young American swimmer Johnny Weissmuller. Using the flutter kick Duke had made famous, Weissmuller broke Duke's existing Olympic record with a speed of 59 seconds in the 100-meter freestyle. Duke accepted the second-place silver medal with a **gracious** smile.

Duke kept training, swimming, and surfing. He thought he had a good chance of beating Weissmuller in the 1928 Olympic Games in Amsterdam, Netherlands, but Duke was sidelined by illness. By the end of his Olympic career in 1932 at age forty-one, Duke had won three gold medals, two silver medals, and one bronze.

To Duke, surfing was a way of life, and one day in 1925 in Southern California he proved that surfboards could also save lives.

Big surf was expected at Corona del Mar, and Duke and two friends had spent the night sleeping on the beach. While checking out the huge, green waves in the foggy morning, Duke noticed a fishing boat making its way close to the coast. Suddenly a great wave curled forward and capsized the boat.

Grabbing his board, Duke sprang into action. He paddled out into the raging ocean and dragged four drowning fishermen onto his surfboard. He commanded the panicked men to lock their arms around his board. The surfboard **somersaulted** and then bounced into the shallows. Duke ran

back into the wild water, searching out the feeble calls for help, pulling fishermen onto his board and taking them in to shore. His friends also entered the wild sea on their boards, searching for survivors.

Duke saved eight people that day and his friends rescued four. Saddened that they had not saved everyone, Duke hurried from the beach before he could be thanked and before news reporters arrived. Later, the actions of Duke and his friends were described as "the most superhuman rescue act and finest display of surf-riding ever seen in the world." Duke was pleased when surfboards became **standard equipment** on emergency rescue trucks and at lifeguard towers.

CHAPTER SEVEN

DUKE'S DREAM

Duke moved back to his island home in 1930. He had done so much to promote Hawai'i and surfing around the world, people insisted there should be a place of honor for him at home. Friends encouraged Duke to run for public office as sheriff of Honolulu. In 1934, he won easily, and he remained Honolulu's sheriff for twenty-six years.

In 1940, when he was fifty, Duke married Nadine Alexander. Twenty years earlier, as a teenager in Boston, she had fallen in love with his picture. When an opportunity to teach dancing in Hawai'i came along in 1938, Nadine jumped at the chance. One of Duke's brothers eventually introduced them, and it was love at first sight.

Hawai'i became the fiftieth state of the United States in 1959, and the sheriff's position was abolished. Duke then became the official state of Hawai'i Ambassador of Aloha. He welcomed politicians, celebrities, and other **distinguished** guests to Hawai'i and **officiated** at countless events and celebrations.

Duke thought of surfing as Hawai'i's gift to the world, and he never stopped promoting the sport. In his lifetime Duke saw surfing grow into a multibillion-dollar **pastime** enjoyed by millions. He loved watching young surfers discover the thrill of riding the waves.

Duke's dream, yet to be fulfilled, was that one day surfing would be an event in the Olympic Games and that surfers would compete for

Olympic gold in the thundering ocean waves.

Duke Paoa Kahanamoku, "the Father of Modern Surfing," died on January 22, 1968, at the age of seventy-seven. He was the world's greatest waterman and the twentieth century's most influential surfer. Just as important, Duke will always be remembered for his kindness and modesty, good sportsmanship, and love of life. As a fellow surfer said, "No matter what he did, he spread aloha."

DUKE'S CREED OF ALOHA

In Hawai'i we greet friends,
loved ones or strangers with Aloha,
which means with love.
Aloha is the key word to the universal
spirit of real hospitality,
which makes Hawai'i renowned
as the world's center
of understanding and fellowship.
Try meeting or leaving people
with Aloha.
You'll be surprised by their reaction.
I believe it and this is my creed.
Aloha to you.

TIMELINE

1890 August 24: Born in Honolulu, Hawai'i

1900 Organic Act makes citizens of Republic of Hawai'i citizens of the United States

1910 Hawaiian Amateur Athletic Union created

1911 Organized Hui Nalu, Club of the Waves

August 12: First Amateur Athletic Union-Hawai'i sanctioned swim meet held in Honolulu Harbor; broke world records in 50-yard, 100-yard, and 220-yard freestyle races

1912 Olympic Games in Stockholm, Sweden; won gold medal in 100-meter freestyle race and silver medal in 4 x 200-meter freestyle relay

Introduced surfing to United States east coast

1914-1915 Introduced surfing to Australia and New Zealand

1915-1932 Helped popularize surfing and swimming in California

1916 Olympic Games in Berlin, Germany, canceled

1917 Rode monster wave in Waikiki for one and three-quarter miles

1918 Swam in exhibitions to raise money for Liberty

Loan War Bonds to support US efforts in World War I

1920   Olympic Games in Antwerp, Belgium; won gold medals in 100-meter freestyle race and 4 x 200-meter freestyle relay

1922-1930   Lived in Los Angeles, California; played small parts in movies

1924   Olympic Games in Paris, France; won silver medal in 100-meter freestyle race

1925   Rescued eight people on surfboard at Corona del Mar, California

1932   Olympic Games in Los Angeles, California; won bronze medal as alternate member of water polo team

1934-1960   Served as Sheriff of City and County of Honolulu

1940   August 2: Married Nadine Alexander

1956   Attended Olympic Games in Melbourne, Australia, as official US representative; recommended surfing as an Olympic event

1959   Hawai'i became fiftieth state of the United States

1960   Appointed official state of Hawai'i Ambassador of Aloha

1964 Honored as Sports Champion of the Century at New York World's Fair

1965 December: First Duke Kahanamoku Invitational Surfing Championships held at Sunset Beach, Oʻahu, Hawaiʻi

1965-1966 One of the first group inducted into International Swimming Hall of Fame and Surfing Hall of Fame

1968 January 22: Died in Honolulu

January 27: Thousands attended Waikiki Beach funeral

1969 Plaque and bust dedicated at Huntington Beach, California

1984 Inducted into US Olympic Hall of Fame

1990 Statue dedicated at Waikiki Beach, Hawaiʻi

1994 Statue dedicated at Freshwater Beach, Sydney, Australia

First name inscribed in Huntington Beach Surfing Walk of Fame

1999 Named Surfer of the Century by *Surfer* magazine

2002 August 24: Duke Kahanamoku commemorative stamp issued by United States Postal Service

GLOSSARY

accompanied (ah-COME-puh-need) *verb* to go along with someone

adrenaline (ah-DREN-ah-lin) *noun* a chemical released in the body of someone who is feeling great excitement or fear, which increases their heart rate and energy

amateur (AM-uh-chur) *noun* someone who participates in an activity for the fun of it rather than for pay

ambitious (am-BISH-us) *adjective* having a will to be successful, powerful, famous, or wealthy

attorney (ah-TUR-nee) *noun* a lawyer

chaperone (SHAP-er-own) *noun* a person who watches over children or other people to keep them safe

contribution (KON-treh-BU-shun) *noun* money or services given to someone or to a cause

crawl stroke (krawl stroke) *noun* a swimming stroke that involves the swimmer pulling the water with their arms and hands while performing a continuous fluid kicking motion. The swimmer's face remains face down in the water and turns to breathe in between arm strokes

cult (kult) *noun* a small group of people who follow extreme religious practices

descendant (dee-SEN-dent) *noun* a person who came from a certain group of people who lived before them

distinguished (dis-TING-wished) *adjective* standing out because of an achievement

equipment (ee-KWIP-ment) *noun* materials or supplies used for a specific activity

exhibition (eks-hee-BIH-shun) *noun* a public event that showcases the participants' skills and abilities

feverishly (FEE-ver-ish-lee) *adverb* an intense emotion related to feelings of anticipation and excitement

flexible (FLEKS-ee-bull) *adjective* capable of bending without breaking

frequency (FREE-kwen-see) *noun* the number of waves that travel past a given point in a period of time

gangway (GANG-way) *noun* a structure people walk across to board a ship

gracious (GRAY-shus) *adjective* showing grace, kindness, politeness

humiliated (hew-MILL-ee-ate-ed) *adjective* experiencing feelings of embarrassment and shame

Kelly Slater (kel-LEE slay-TUR; 1972-) *person* an award-winning American professional surfer

longboard (long-bored) *noun* a surfboard that ranges between nine and twelve feet long, with a rounded nose. Longboards provide greater stability than other boards, which makes them ideal for beginner surfers

maneuver (ma-NEW-vur) *noun* a specific or skillful move

oath (OWTH) *noun* a pledge someone makes to do something

obliged (o-BLIGED) *verb* to agree to do something that's been asked of you

officiate (o-FISH-ee-ate) *verb* to oversee a ceremony or contest

Olympic Games (Oh-LIM-pik gayms) *noun* an international athletic competition held once every four years

ordeal (OR-deel) *noun* an experience that is difficult or troublesome

pagan (PAY-gan) *noun* a person who follows religious practices outside the major world religions

pastime (PAS-time) *noun* an enjoyable hobby or activity

pentathlon (pen-TATH-lon) *noun* an athletic contest consisting of five different challenges

posthumously (post-HEW-most-lee) *adjective* done after a person's death

propelled (PRO-pelled) *verb* pushed or moved forward

prowess (PROW-ess) *noun* great skill

qualify (KWA-lif-eye) *verb* to have the skills necessary for a certain task or opportunity

recognition (REK-og-nish-on) *noun* the act of recognizing or acknowledging something

reprimanded (rep-ree-MAN-ded) *verb* to speak in an angry way to someone who has done something wrong

sarcastic (sar-KAS-tik) *adjective* mocking or insulting

sensational (sen-SAY-shun-al) *adjective* amazing or excellent

somersaulted (SUM-mur-SAL-ted) *verb* to turn or flip forward or backward

stammered (STAM-murred) *verb* to speak in an uncertain way, with pauses and repetition

standard (STAND-erd) *adjective* similar and consistent

tandem (TAN-dum) *noun* working together at the same time

triumphant (try-UM-fant) *adjective* victorious

virtually (VER-chew-al-lee) *adverb* nearly

vocational (voh-KAY-shun-al) *adjective* related to a specific set of skills or a trade

wharves (warvs) *noun* structures where ships can dock and load or unload cargo

TEXT SOURCES

Brennan, Joseph L. *Duke: The Life Story of Duke Kahanamoku.* Honolulu, HI: Ku Pa'a Publishing, 1994.

———. *Duke Kahanamoku: Hawaii's Golden Man.* Honolulu, HI: Hogarth Press, 1974.

Finney, Ben R. and Houston, James D. *Surfing: A History of the Ancient Hawaiian Sport.* Rohnert Park, CA: Pomegranate Artbooks, 1996.

Hall, Sandra Kimberley. *Duke: A Great Hawaiian.* Honolulu, HI: Bess Press, 2004.

Hall, Sandra Kimberley and Greg Ambrose. *Memories of Duke: The Legend Comes to Life.* Honolulu, HI: Bess Press, 1995.

Kahanamoku, Duke Paoa, and Brennan, Joe. *Duke Kahanamoku's World of Surfing.* New York: Grosset & Dunlap, 1968.

Timmons, Grady. *Waikiki Beachboy.* Honolulu, HI: Editions Limited, 1989.

Young, Nat. *The History of Surfing.* Angourie, Australia: Palm Beach Press, 1983.

QUOTATION SOURCES

Several quotations in the book are from interviews with Duke Kahanamoku conducted by Joseph L. Brennan, Kahanamoku's longtime friend and biographer.

p. 10: "I'd like . . . got it." Quoted in Brennan, *Duke: The Life Story of Duke Kahanamoku,* p. 22.

p. 20: "What are . . . clocks?" Ibid., p. 33.

"Coming down!" Kahanamoku family Website: http://www.hawaiianswimboat.com

p. 26: "Hello, . . . joining us." Quoted in Brennan, *Duke: The Life Story of Duke Kahanamoku,* p. 40.

"Waiter, please . . . Kahanamoku." Ibid.

pp. 34–35: "Jimmy . . . care of." Duke Kahanamoku interview, 1965. Reported in *Honolulu Star-Bulletin,* August 23, 1965.

p. 36: "Kahanamoku wanted . . . starting platform." Quoted in Brennan, *Duke: The Life Story of Duke Kahanamoku,* p. 52.

"Where've you . . . been sleeping." Ibid.

p. 45: "Man overboard!" Brennan, *Duke: The Life Story of Duke Kahanamoku,* p. 71.

p. 47: "unusually ... extremities," Quoted in Brennan, *Duke: The Life Story of Duke Kahanamoku,* p. 87.

p. 50: "for the ... sport." Athletes' Olympic Oath. International Olympic Committee Website: http://www.olympic.org/uk/utilities/ faq_detail_uk.asp?rdo_cat=10_39_0.

p. 59: "the most ... the world." Newport Beach, California, Chief of Police J. A. Porter, June 15, 1925. Quoted in Brennan, *Duke: The Life Story of Duke Kahanamoku,* p. 156.

p. 62: "No matter ... spread aloha." Rabbit Kekai. *Surfer* magazine, vol. 40, no. 10, October 1999.

p. 63: Duke's Creed of Aloha. Message printed on back of Kahanamoku's business cards.

SIDEBAR SOURCES

A BRIEF HISTORY OF HAWAI'I

Crowe, Ellie. *Hawaii, A Pictorial Celebration*. Photographs by Elan Penn. New York: Sterling Publishing, 2007.

Crowe, Ellie and William Crowe. *Exploring Lost Hawai'i: Places of Power, History, Mystery & Magic*. Honolulu, HI: Island Heritage, 2005.

Library of Congress Teacher Resources Classroom Presentation. "Immigration Japanese." https://www.loc.gov/teachers/classroommaterials/presentationsandactivities/presentations/immigration/japanese2.html

National Geographic Society Education Teaching Resources. "This Day in Geographic History July 6 1887: Bayonet Constitution." https://www.nationalgeographic.org/thisday/jul6/bayonet-constitution

JIM THORPE

Encyclopedia.com. "Jim Thorpe Facts Information Pictures." https://www.encyclopedia.com/people/sports-and-games/sports-biographies/jim-thorpe

Prague Oklahoma. "Jim Thorpe." Accessed May 2018.
http://praguechamber.org/jim-thorpe/

ThoughtCo. "Biography of Jim Thorpe." Accessed
May 2018. https://www.thoughtco.com/
jim-thorpe-1779819

HOW SURFBOARDS ARE MADE

360 Guide. "Board Construction - How Surfboards
are Made." Accessed May 2018. http://360guide.
info/surfing/surfboard-construction.
html#axzz5HDOHjM4G

HawaiiHistory.org. "Ancient Boards." Accessed April
2018. http://www.hawaiihistory.org/index.cfm?fuse-
action=ig.page&PageID=391

THE OLYMPIC GAMES

Benagh, Jim. "The History of the Olympic Games."
Scholastic.com. Accessed April 2018. https://www.
scholastic.com/teachers/articles/teaching-content/
history-olympic-games/

History.com. "The Olympic Games." Accessed April 2018.
https://www.history.com/topics/olympic-games

Pyeong Chang 2018. "From Ancient to Modern: the
History of the Olympic Games." Posted February 16,
2016. https://www.pyeongchang2018.com/en/blog/
From-Ancient-to-Modern-The-History-of-the-

Olympic-Games

Your Dictionary. "Pierre de Coubertin Facts-Biography." Accessed April 2018. http://biography.yourdictionary.com/pierre-de-coubertin

HOW TO SURF

Surfing Waves. "Your First Surfboard." Accessed July 2018. http://www.surfing-waves.com/beginner_surfboard.htm

The Surfing Site. "Surfing Tips & Techniques for the Beginner Surfer." Accessed May 2018. http://www.thesurfingsite.com/How-to-Surf.html

RECOMMENDED FURTHER READING

Fiction books are marked with an asterisk.

THE OLYMPICS AND OLYMPIC ATHLETES

Bruchac, Joseph. *Jim Thorpe's Bright Path*. New York: Lee & Low Books, 2004.

Bruchac, Joseph. *Jim Thorpe: Original All-American*. New York: Dial Books, 2006.

Feinstein, John. *Rush for the Gold: Mystery at the Olympics*. The Sports Beat. New York: Knopf Books for Young Readers, 2012.

Hermen, Gail. *What Are the Summer Olympics?* What Was?. New York: Penguin, 2016.

Spence, Kelly. *Yusra Mardini: Refugee Hero and Olympic Swimmer*. Remarkable Lives Revealed. New York: Crabtree Publishing, 2018.

Time-Life Books. *The Olympics: Moments That Made History*. Tampa, FL: Time Inc. Books, 2016.

HAWAIʻI

*Aslan, Austin. *The Islands at the End of the World*. New York: Random House, 2015.